CALIFORNIA
NATIVE AMERICAN TRIBES

ATSUGEWI TRIBE

by

Mary Null Boulé

Book Two in a series of twenty-six

Dear Reader,

You will find an outline of this chapter's important topics at the back of the booklet. It is there for you to use in writing a report or giving an oral report on this tribe.

If you first read the booklet completely, then you can use the outline as a guide to write your report in your own words, instead of copying sentences from the chapter.

Good luck, read carefully,
and use your own words.

MNB

CALIFORNIA
NATIVE AMERICAN TRIBES

ATSUGEWI TRIBE

by
Mary Null Boulé

Illustrated by
Daniel Liddell

Merryant Publishing
Vashon, Washington

Book Number Two in a series of twenty-six

1

This series is dedicated to Virginia Harding, whose editing expertise and friendship brought this project to fruition.

Library of Congress #92-061897

ISBN: 1-877599-26-3

Copyright © 1992, Merryant Publishing

7615 S.W. 257th St., Vashon, WA 98070.

FOREWORD

Native American people of the United States are often living their lives away from major cities and away from what we call the mainstream of life. It is, then, interesting to learn of the important part these remote tribal members play in our everyday lives.

More than 60% of our foods come from the ancient Native American's diet. Farming methods of today also can be traced back to how tribal women grew crops of corn and grain. Many of our present day ideas of democracy have been taken from tribal governments. Even some 1,500 Native American words are found in our English language today.

Fur traders bought furs from tribal hunters for small amounts of money, sold them to Europeans and Asians for a great deal of money, and became rich. Using their money to buy land and to build office buildings, some traders started business corporations which are now the base of our country's economy.

There has never been enough credit given to these early Americans who took such good care of our country when it was still in their care. The time has come to realize tribal contributions to our society today and to give Native Americans not only the credit, but the respect due them.

Mary Boulé

A-frame cradle for girls; tule matting. Tubatulabal tribe.

GENERAL INFORMATION

Out of Asia, many thousands of years ago, came Wanderers. Some historians think they were the first people to set foot on our western hemisphere. These Wanderers had walked, step by step, onto our part of the earth while hunting and gathering food. They probably never even knew they had moved from one continent to another as they made their way across a land bridge, a narrow strip of land between Siberia and what is now Russia, and the state of Alaska.

Historians do not know exactly how long ago the Wanderers might have crossed the land bridge. Some of them say 35,000 years ago. What historians do know is that these people slowly moved down onto land that we now call the United States of America. Today it would be very hard to follow their footsteps, for the land bridge has been covered with sea water since the thawing of the ice age.

Those Wanderers who made their way to California were very lucky, indeed. California was a land with good weather most of the year and was filled with plenty of plant and animal foods for them to eat.

The Wanderers who became California's Native Americans did not organize into large tribes like the rest of the North American tribes. Instead, they divided into groups, or tribelets, sometimes having as many as 250 people. A tribelet could number as few as three, to as many as thirty villages located close to each other. Some tribelets had only one chief, a leader who lived in the largest village. Many tribes had a chief for each village. Some leaders had no real power but were thought to be wise. Tribal members always listened with respect to what their chief had to say.

From 20 to 100 people could be living in one village, which usually had several houses. In most cases, these groups of people were related to each other. From five to ten people of one family lived in one house. For instance, a mother, a father, two or three children, a grandmother, or aunt or daughter-in-law might live together.

Village members together would own the land important to them for their well-being. Their land might include oak trees with precious acorns, streams and rivers, and plants which were good to eat. Streams and rivers were especially important to a tribe's quality of life. Water drew animals to it; that meant more food for the tribe to eat. Fish were a good source of food, and traveling by boat was often easier than walking long distances. Water was needed in every part of tribal life.

Village and tribelet land was carefully guarded. Each group knew exactly where the boundaries of its land were found. Boundaries were known by landmarks such as mountains or rivers, or they might also be marked by poles planted in the ground. Some boundary lines were marked by rocks, or by objects placed there by tribal members. The size of a territory had to be large enough to supply food to every person living there.

The California tribes spoke many languages. Sometimes villages close together even had a problem understanding one another. This meant that each group had to be sure of the boundaries of other tribes around them when gathering food. It would not be wise to go against the boundaries and the customs of neighbors. The Native Americans found if they respected the boundaries of their neighbors, not so many wars had to be fought. California tribes, in spite of all their differences, were not as warlike as other tribes in our country.

Not only did the California tribes speak different languages, but their members also differed in size. Some tribes were very tall, almost six feet tall. The shortest people came from the Yuki tribe which had territory in what is now Mendocino County. They measured only about 5'2" tall. All Native Americans, regardless of size, had strong, straight black hair and dark brown eyes.

TRADE

Trading between tribes was an important part of life. Inland tribes had large animal hides that coastal tribes wanted. By trading the hides to coastal groups, inland tribes would receive fish and shells, which they in turn wanted. Coastal tribes also wanted minerals and rocks mined in the mountains by inland tribes. Obsidian rock from the northern mountains was especially wanted for arrowheads. There were, as well, several minerals, mined in the inland mountains, which could be made into the colorful body paints needed for religious ceremonies.

Southern tribes particularly wanted steatite from the Gabrielino tribe. Steatite, or soapstone, was a special metal which allowed heat to spread evenly through it. This made it a good choice to be used for cooking pots and flat frying pans. It could be carved into bowls because of its softness and could be decorated by carving designs into it. Steatite came from Catalina Island in the Coastal Gabrielino territory. Gabrielinos found steatite to be a fine trading item to offer for the acorns, deerskins, or obsidian stone they needed.

When people had no items to trade but needed something, they used small strings of shells for money. The small dentalium shells, which came from the far distant Northwest coast, had great value. Strings of dentalia usually served as money in the Northern California tribes, although some dentalia was used in the Central California tribes.

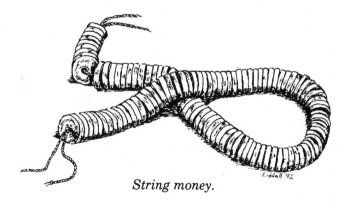

String money.

In southern California clam shells were broken and holes were bored through the center of each piece. Then the pieces were rounded and polished with sandstone and strung into strings for money. These were not thought to be as valuable as dentalia.

Strings of shell money were measured by tattoo marks on the trader's lower arm or hand.

Here is a sample of shell value:

A house, three strings
A fishing place, one to three strings
Land with acorn-bearing oak trees, one to five strings

A great deal of rock and stone was traded among the tribes for making tools. Arrows had to have sharp-edged stone for tips. The best stone for arrow tips was obsidian (volcanic glass) because, when hit properly, it broke off into flakes with very sharp edges. California tribes considered obsidian to be the most valuable rock for trading.

Some tribes had craftsmen who made knives with wooden handles and obsidian blades. Often the handles were decorated with carvings. Such knives were good for trading purposes. Stone mortars and pestles, used by the women for grinding grains into flour, were good trading items.

BASKETS & POTTERY

California tribal women made beautiful baskets. The Pomo and Chumash baskets, what few are left, show us that the women of those tribes might have been some of the finest basketmakers in the world. Baskets were used for gathering and storing food, for carrying babies, and even for hauling water. In emergencies, such as flooding waters, sometimes children, women, and tribal belongings crossed the swollen rivers and streams in huge, woven baskets! Baskets were so tightly woven that not a drop of water could leak from them.

Baskets also made fine cooking pots. Very hot rocks were taken from a fire and tossed around inside baskets with a looped tree branch until food in the basket was cooked.

Most baskets were made to do a certain job, but some baskets were designed for their beauty alone and were excellent for trading. Older women of a tribe would teach young girls how to weave baskets.

Pottery was not used by many California tribes. What little there was seems to have been made by those tribes living near to the Navaho and Mohave tribes of Arizona, and it shows their style. For example, pottery of the California tribes did not have much decoration and was usually a dull red color. Designs were few and always in yellow.

Ohlone hunter wearing deerskin camouflage.

Long thin coils of clay were laid one on top the other. Then the coils were smoothed between a wooden paddle and a small stone to shape the bowl. Pottery from California Native Americans has been described as light weight and brittle (easily broken), probably because of the kind of clay soil found in California.

HUNTING & FISHING

Tribal men spent much of their time making hunting and fishing tools. Bows and arrows were built with great care, to make them shoot as accurately as possible. Carelessly made hunting weapons caused fewer animals to be killed and people then had less food to eat.

Bows made by men of Southern California tribes were made long and narrow. In the northern part of the state bows were a little shorter, thinner, and wider than those of their northern neighbors. Size and thickness of bows depended on the size trees growing in a tribe's territory. The strongest bows were wrapped with sinew, the name given to animal tendons. Sinew is strong and elastic like a rubber band.

Arrows were made in many sizes and shapes, depending on their use. For hunting larger animals, a two-piece arrow was used. The front piece of the arrow shaft was made so that it would remain in the animal, even if the back part was

9

removed or broken off. The arrowhead, or point, was wrapped to the front piece of the shaft. This kind of arrow was also used in wars.

Young boys used a simple wooden arrow with the end sharpened to a point. With this they could hunt small animals like birds and rabbits. The older men of the tribe taught boys how to make their own arrows, how to aim properly, and how to repair broken weapons.

Tribal men spent many hours making and mending fishing nets. The string used in making nets often came from the fibers of plants. These fibers were twisted to make them strong and tough, then knotted into netting. Fences, or weirs, that had one small opening for fish, were built across streams. As the fish swam through the opening they would be caught in netting or harpooned by a waiting fisherman.

Hooks, if used at all, were cut from shells. Mostly hooks could be found when the men fished in large lakes or when catching trout in high mountain areas. Hooks were attached to heavy plant fiber string.

Dip nets, made of netting attached to branches that were bent into a circle, were used to catch fish swimming near shore. Dip nets had long handles so the fishermen could reach deep into the water.

Sometimes a mild poison was placed on the surface of shallow water. This confused the fish and caused them to float to the surface of the water, where they could be scooped up by a waiting fisherman. Not enough poison was used to make humans ill.

Not all fishing was done from the shore. California tribes used two kinds of boats when fishing. Canoes, dug out of one half a log, were useful for river fishing. These were square at each end, round on the bottom, and very heavy. Some of them were well-finished, often even having a carved seat in them.

Today we think of "balsa" as a very lightweight wood, but in Spanish, the word balsa means "raft". That is why Spanish explorers called the Native American canoes, made from tule reeds, "balsa" boats.

Balsa boats were made of bundled tule reeds and were used throughout most of California. They made into safe, light-weight boats for lake and river use. Usually the balsa canoe had a long, tightly tied bundle of tule for the boat bottom and one bundle for each side of the canoe. The front of the canoe was higher than the back. Balsa boats could be steered with a pole or with a paddle, like a raft.

Men did most of the fishing, women were in charge of gathering grasses, seeds, and acorns for food. After the food was collected, it was either eaten right away or made ready for winter storage.

Except for a few southern groups, California tribes had permanent villages where they lived most of the year. They also had food-gathering places they returned to each year to collect acorns, salt, fish, and other foods not found near their villages.

FOOD

Many different kinds of plant food grew wild in California in the days before white people arrived. Berries and other plant foods grew in the mountains. Forests offered the local tribes everything from pine nuts to animals.

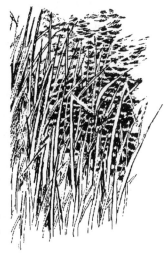

Native Americans found streams full of fish for much of the year. Inland fresh water lakes had large tule reeds growing along their shores. Tule could be eaten as food when plants were young and tender. More important, however, tule was used in making fabric for clothes and for building boats and houses. Tule was probably the most useful plant the California Native Americans found growing wild in their land.

Like all deserts, the one in southern California had little water or fish, but small animals and cactus plants made good food for the local tribes. They moved from place to place harvesting whatever was ripe. Tribal members always knew when and where to find the best food in their territory.

Acorns were the main source of food for all California tribes. Acorn flour was as important to the California Native Americans as wheat is to us today. Five types of California oak trees produced acorns that could be eaten. Those from black oak and tanbark oak seem to have been the favorite kinds.

Since some acorns tasted better than others, the tastiest ones were collected first. If harvest of the favorite acorn was poor some years, then less tasty acorns had to be eaten all winter long.

So important were acorns to California Indians that most tribes built their entire year around them. Acorn harvest marked the beginning of their calendar year. Winter was counted as so many months after acorn harvest, and summer was counted by the number of months before the next acorn harvest.

Acorn harvest ceremonies usually were the biggest events of the year. Most celebrations took place in mid-October and included dancing, feasts, games of chance, and reunions with relatives. Harvest festivals lasted for many days. They were a time of joy for everyone.

The annual acorn gathering lasted two to three weeks. Young boys climbed the oak trees to shake branches; some men used long poles to knock acorns to the ground. Women loaded the nuts into large cone-shaped burden baskets and carried them to a central place where they were put in the sun to dry.

Once the acorns were dried, the women carried them back to the tribe's permanent villages. There they lined special basket-like storage granaries with strong herbs to keep insects away, then stored the acorns inside. Granaries were placed on stilts to keep animals from getting into them and were kept beside tribal houses.

Preparing acorns for each meal was also the women's job. Shells were peeled by hitting the acorns with a stone hammer on an anvil (flat) stone. Meat from the nut was then laid on a stone mortar. A mortar was usually a large stone with a slight dip on its surface. Sometimes the mortar had a bottomless basket, called a hopper, glued to its top. This kept the acorn meat from sliding off the mortar as it was beaten. The meat was then pounded with a long stone pestle. Acorn flour was scraped away from the hopper's sides with a soaproot fiber brush during this process.

From there the flour was put into an open-worked basket and sifted. A fine flour came through the bottom of the basket, while the larger pieces were put back in the mortar for more pounding.

The most important process came after the acorn flour was sifted. Acorn flour has a very bitter-tasting tannin in it. This bitter taste was removed by a method called leaching. Many tribes leached the flour by first scooping out a hollow in sand near water. The hollow was lined with leaves to keep the flour from washing away. A great deal of hot water was poured through the flour to wash out (leach) the bitterness. Sometimes the flour was put into a basket for the leaching process, instead of using sand and leaves.

Finally the acorn flour was ready to be cooked. To make mush, heated stones were placed in the basket with the flour. A looped tree branch or two long sticks were used to toss the hot rocks around so the basket would not burn. When the mush had boiled, it could be eaten. If the flour and water mixture was baked in an earthen oven, it became a kind of bread. Early explorers wrote that it was very tasty.

Historians have estimated that one family would eat from 1500 to 2000 pounds of acorn flour a year. One reason California native Americans did not have to plant seeds and raise crops was because there were so many acorns for them to harvest each year.

Whether they ate fish or shellfish or plant food or animal meat, nature supplied more than enough food for the Native Americans who lived in California long ago. Many believed their good fortune in having fine weather and plenty to eat came from being good to their gods.

RELIGION

Tribal members had strong beliefs in the power of spirits or gods around them. Each tribe was different, but all felt the importance of never making a spirit angry with them. For that reason a celebration to thank the spirit-gods for treating them well, took place before each food gathering and before each hunting trip, and after each food harvest.

Usually spiritual powers were thought to belong to birds or animals. Most California tribespeople felt bears were very wicked and should not be eaten. But Coyote seems to have been a kind leader who helped them if they were in trouble, even though he seems to have been a bit naughty at times. Eagle was thought to be very powerful and good to native Americans. In some tribes, Eagle was almost as powerful as Sun.

Tribes placed importance on different gods, according to the tribe's needs. Rain gods were the most important spirits to desert tribes. Weather gods, who might bring less rain or warmer temperatures, were important to northern tribes. A great many groups felt there were gods for each of the winds: North, South, East and West. The four directions were usually included in their ceremonial dances and were used as part of the decorations on baskets, pots, and even tools.

Animals were not only worshipped and believed to be spirit-gods, like Deer or Antelope, but tribal members felt there was a personal animal guardian for each one of them. If a tribal member had a deer as guardian, then that person could never kill a deer or eat deer meat.

California Native Americans believed in life after death. This made them very respectful of death and very fearful of angering a dead person. Once someone died, the name of the dead person could never again be said aloud. Since it was easy to accidentally say a name aloud, the name was usually given to a new baby. Then the dead person would not become angry.

Shamans were thought to be the keepers of religious beliefs and to have the ability to talk directly to spirit-gods. It was the job of a village shaman to cure sick people, and to speak to the gods about the needs of the people. Some tribes had several kinds of shamans in one village. One shaman did curing, one scared off evil spirits, while another took care of hunters.

Not all shamans were nice, so people greatly feared their power. However, if shamans had no luck curing sick people or did not bring good luck in hunting, the people could kill them. Most shamans were men, but in a few tribes, women were doctors.

Most California tribal myths have been lost to history because they were spoken and never written down. The legends were told and retold on winter nights around the home fires. Sadly, these were forgotten after the missionaries brought Christianity to California and moved tribal members into the missions.

A few stories still remain, however. It is thought by historians that northwest California tribes were the only ones not to have a myth on how they were created. They did not feel that the world was made and prepared for human beings. Instead, their few remaining stories usually tell of mountain peaks or rivers in their own territory.

The central California tribes had creation stories of a great flood where there was only water on earth. They tell of how man was made from a bit of mud that a turtle brought up from the bottom of the water.

Many southwest tribes believed there was a time of no sky or water. They told of two clouds appearing which finally became Sky and Earth.

Throughout California, however, all tribes had myths that told of Eagle as the leader, Coyote as chief assistant, and of less powerful spirits like Falcon or Hawk.

Costumes for religious ceremonies often imitated these animals they worshipped or feared. Much time was spent in making the dance costumes as beautiful as possible. Red woodpecker feathers were so brilliant a color they were used to decorate religious headdresses, necklaces, or belts. Deerskin clothing was fringed so shell beads could be attached to each thin strip of leather.

Eagle feathers were felt to be the most sacred of religious objects. Sometimes they were made into whole robes.

Religious feather charm.

Usually, though, the feathers were used just for decorations. All these costumes were valuable to the people of each tribe. The village chief was in charge of taking care of the costumes, and there was terrible punishment for stealing them. Clothing worn everyday was not fancy like costuming for rituals.

Willow bark skirt.

CLOTHING

Central and southern California's fine weather made regular clothes not really very important to the Native Americans. The children and men went naked most of the year, but most women wore a short apron-like skirt. These skirts were usually made in two pieces, front and back aprons, with fringes cut into the bottom edges. Often the skirt was made from the inner bark of trees, shredded and gathered on a cord. Sometimes the skirt was made from tule or grass.

In northern California and in rainy or windy weather elsewhere in the state, animal-skin blankets were worn by both men and women. They were used like a cape and wrapped around the body. Sometimes the cape was put over one shoulder and under the other arm, then tied in front. All kinds of skins were used; deer, otter, wildcat, but sea-otter fur was thought to be the best. If the skin was from a small animal, it was cut into strips and woven together into a fabric. At night the cape became a blanket to keep the person warm.

Because of the rainy weather in northern California, the women wore basket caps all the time. Women of the central and south tribes wore caps only when carrying heavy loads, where the forehead had to be used as support. Then a cap helped keep too much weight from being placed on the forehead.

Most California people went barefoot in their villages. For journeys into rough land, going to war, wood gathering, or in colder weather, the tribesmen in central and northwest California wore a one-piece soft shoe with no extra sole, which went high up on the leg.

Southern California tribespeople, however, wore sandals most of the time, wearing high, soled moccasins only when they traveled long distances or into the mountains. Leggings of skin were worn in snow, and moccasins were sometimes lined with grass for more comfort and warmth.

VILLAGE LIFE

Houses of the California tribes were made of materials found in their area. Usually they were round with domed roofs. Except for a few tribes, a house floor was dug into the earth a few feet. This was wise, for it made the home warmer in winter and cooler in summer. It also meant that less material was needed to make house walls.

Framework for the walls was made from bendable branches tied to support poles. Some frames of the houses were covered with earth and grass. Others were covered with large slabs of redwood or pine bark. Central California

Split-stick clapper, rhythm instrument. Hupa tribe.

villagers made large woven mats of tule reed to cover the tops and sides of houses. In the warmer southern area, brush and smaller pieces of bark were used for house walls.

Most California Native American villages had a building called a sweathouse, where the men could be found when they were not hunting, fishing or traveling. It was a very important place for the men, who used it rather like a clubhouse. They could sweat and then scrape themselves clean with curved ribs of deer. The sweathouse was smaller than a family house. Normally it had a center pole framework with a firepit on the ground next to the pole. When the fire was lit, some smoke was allowed to escape through a hole at the top of the roof; however, most was trapped inside the building. Smoke and heat were the main reasons for having a sweathouse. Both were believed to be a way to purify tribal members' bodies. Sweathouse walls were mainly hard-packed earth. The heat produced was not a steam heat but came from a wood-fed fire.

In the center of most villages was a large house that often had no walls, just a roof held up with poles. It was here that religious dances and rituals were held, or visitors were entertained.

Dances were enjoyed and were performed with great skill. Music, usually only rhythm instruments, accompanied the dances. For some reason California Native Americans did not use drums to create rhythms for their dances. Three different kinds of rattles were used by California tribes.

One type, split-clap sticks, created rhythm for dancing. These were usually a length of cane (a hollow stick) split in half lengthwise for about two-thirds of its length. The part still uncut was tightly wound with cord so it would not split all the way. The stick was held at the tied end in one hand and hit against the palm of the other hand to make its sound.

19

A pebble-filled moth cocoon made rhythm for shaman duties. These could range from calling on spirits to cure illnesses, to performing dances to bring rain. Probably the best sounds to beat rhythm for songs and dances came from bundles of deer hooves tied together on a stick. These rattles have a hollow, warm sound.

The only really "musical" instrument found in California was a flute made of reed that was played by blowing across the edge of one end. Melodies were not played on any of these instruments. Most North American Indians sang their songs rather than playing melodies on music instruments.

Special songs were sung for each event. There were songs for healing sick people, songs for success in hunting, war, or marriage. Women sang acorn-grinding songs and lullabies. Songs were sung in sorrow for the dead and during story-telling times. Group singing, with a leader, was the favorite kind of singing. Most songs were sung by all tribe members, but religious songs had to be sung by a special group. It was important that sacred songs not be changed through the years. If a mistake was made while singing sacred music, the singer could be punished, so only specially trained singers would sing ritual songs.

All songs were very short, some of them only 20 to 30 seconds long. They were made longer by repeating the melodies over and over, or by connecting several songs together. Songs usually told no story, just repeated words or phrases or syllables in patterns.

Song melodies used only one or two notes and harmony was never added. Perhaps that is why mission Indians, at those missions with musician priests, especially loved to sing harmony in the church choirs.

Songs and dances were good methods of passing rich tribal traditions on to the children. It was important to tribal adults that their children understand and love the tribe's heritage.

Children were truly wanted by parents in most tribes and new parents carefully watched their tiny babies day and night, to be sure they stayed warm and dry. Usually a newborn was strapped into a cradle and tied to the mother's back so she could continue to work, yet be near the baby at all times. In some tribes, older children took care of babies of cradle age during the day to give the mother time to do all her work, while grandmothers were often in charge of caring for toddlers.

Children were taught good behavior, traditions, and tribal rules from babyhood, although some tribes were stricter than others. Most of the time parents made their children obey. Young children could be lightly punished, but in many tribes those over six or seven years old were more severely punished if they did not follow the rules.

Just as children do today, Native American youngsters had childhood traditions they followed. For instance, one tribal tradition said that when a baby tooth came out, a child waited until dusk, faced the setting sun and threw the tooth to the west. There is no mention of a generous tooth fairy, however.

Tribal parents were worried that their offspring might not be strong and brave. Some tribes felt one way to make their children stronger was by forcing them to bathe in ice cold water, even in wintertime. Every once in a while, for example, Modoc children were awakened from sleep and taken to a cold lake or stream for a freezing bath.

But if freezing baths at night were hard on young Native Americans, their days were carefree and happy. Children were allowed to play all day, and some tribes felt children did not even have to come to dinner if they didn't want to. In those tribes, children could come to their houses to eat anytime of the day.

The games boys played are not too different from those played today. Swimming, hide and seek among the tule reeds, a form of tetherball with a mud ball tied to a pole, and willow-javelin throwing kept boys busy throughout the day.

Fathers made their sons small bows and arrows, so boys spent much time trying to improve their hunting skills. They practised shooting at frogs or chipmunks. The first animal any boy killed was not touched or eaten by him. Others would carry the kill home to be cooked and eaten by villagers. This tradition taught boys always to share food.

Another hunting tool for boys was a hollowed-out willow branch. This became like a modern day beanshooter, only the Native American boys shot juniper berries instead of beans. Slingshots made good hunting weapons, as well.

Girls and boys shared many games, but girls playing with each other had contests to see who could make a basket the fastest, or they played with dolls made of tule. Together, young boys and girls played a type of ring-around-the-rosie game, climbed mountains, or built mud houses.

As children grew older, the boys followed their fathers and the girls followed their mothers as the adults did their daily work. Children were not trained in the arts of hunting or basketmaking, however, until they became teenagers.

HISTORY

Spanish missionaries, led by Fray Junipero Serra, arrived in California in 1769 to build missions along the coast of California. By 1823, fifty years later, 21 missions had been founded. Almost all of them were very successful, and the Franciscan monks who ran them were proud of how many Native Americans became Christians.

However, all was not as the monks had planned it would be. Native American people had never been around the diseases European white men brought with them. As a result, they had no immunity to such illnesses as measles, small pox, or flu. Too many mission Indians died from white men's diseases.

Historians figure there were 300,000 Native Americans living in California before the missionaries came. The missions show records of 83,000 mission Indians during mission days. By the time the Mexicans took over the missions from the Spanish in 1834, only 20,000 remained alive.

The great California Gold Rush of 1849 was probably another big reason why many of the Native Americans died during that time. White men, staking their claim to tribal lands with gold upon it, thought nothing of killing any California tribesman who tried to keep and protect his territory. Fifty-thousand tribal members died from diseases, bullets, or starvation between the gold Rush Days and 1870. By 1910, only 17,000 California Indians remained.

Although the American government tried to set aside reservations (areas reserved for Native Americans), the land given to the Indians often was not good land. Worse yet, some of the land sacred to tribes, such as burial grounds, was taken over by white people and never given back.

Sadly, mission Indians, when they became Christians, forgot the proud heritage and beliefs they had followed for thousands of years. Many wonderful myths and songs they had passed from one generation to the next, on winter nights so long ago, have been lost forever.

Today some 100,000 people can claim California Native American ancestors, but few pure-blooded tribespeople remain. Our link with the Wanderers, who came from Asia so long ago, has been forever broken.

The bullroarer made a deep, loud sound when whirled above the player's head. Tipai tribe.

Villages were usually built beside a lake, stream, or river. Balsa canoes are on the shore. Tule reeds grow along the edge of the water and are drying on poles on the right side of the picture.

Women preparing food in baskets, sit on tule mats. Tule mats are being tied to the willow pole framework of a house being built by one of the men.

THE ATSUGEWI TRIBE

INTRODUCTION

The Atsugewi (Aht soo gay' wee) were two groups of people. One group was known as the Pine-Tree People. They lived north of Mount Lassen. The second group was called the Juniper-Tree People. They were found on the high desert plain northeast of Mount Lassen. It is thought the name comes from the word "atsuke", the Indian name for a place on Hat Creek. Later on the tribe became known as the Hat Creek tribe.

THE LAND

Atsugewi land had tall mountain peaks and many lakes. Cooler and wetter weather created heavy forests on the west side of the territory. This changed to grasslands and to juniper trees on the drier east side. The boundaries of Atsugewi were never very clear; the tribe always had arguments with the Maidu tribe to the south and the Paiute tribe to the east about where these territory lines were. It is known, however, that Atsugewi people claimed the northern side of Mount Lassen as their area.

THE VILLAGE

Winter villages were built along streams in the lowest land of Atsugewi territory. Even at that lower level, deep snow covered the ground for six months out of the year. Smaller villages had from 3 to 25 earth lodges or bark houses. Sweathouses of prehistory (before white people) time are not described, but it is known that in 1880 village sweathouses were domed-shaped and made of animal skins.

Larger villages were not always located in one spot, but were made up of several clusters of houses. Sometimes the clusters were quite far apart, like today's suburbs which build up around a big city. The best lowland for villages was found in the Dixie and Little valleys, and along part of the Pit River from Horse Creek to Beaver Creek.

VILLAGE LIFE

Each village had its own chief, and there was no overall chief in charge of the whole tribe. Village chiefs, who were usually rich men, had their own followers living near them. A chief often owned much of the land around his village. Well-liked chiefs had power. Some were powerful even in places outside their own villages. Chiefs could not punish people, but could take away their approval of a person, which was just as bad.

Usually a chief listened to what his people wanted, because he felt rather like a father to them. He was there to settle fights among his people and saw to it that fines were paid by troublemakers. He might awaken his villagers at dawn by shouting advice to them. He would tell them to get up early, to work hard, and to gather and store enough food for the long winter ahead. A chief had to set a good example himself by working hard at jobs like hunting, fishing, or making fish nets.

Atsugewi house made of several layers of bark.

It was up to the chief to pay for any feasts given by his village. Even though he was sometimes paid small gifts of food for the use of his land, no large amounts of food were given to him unless a feast was planned. For this reason, the chief was often not the richest man in a village; he had to pay for too many parties.

When the time came for an old chief to step down, it was not always his eldest son who took over the job. Sometimes the best son, or even a cousin, was chosen to be the new chief. Whether or not one of a chief's sons took over for his father, all sons were always specially trained for the job of chief, just in case.

At least once every six days the chief would call a day of rest. Then everyone could stay in the camp or village so women could cook food and men could fix their tools. In wintertime the rest day was usually just before a big hunt, when all the village men went hunting together.

Sometimes men and boys were allowed to perform sweat dances on the day before a big winter hunt. Smokeless wood was burned in the heated sweathouse and men danced alone to see who could stand the highest heat. When they became too hot they would run outside and roll in the snow or dive into icy water. Young women and children usually did not join in this kind of dance.

A village could also have several wealthy men, known as headmen, who spoke for and led a group of close friends. These men could be most kind to their friends if any of them ran out of food. What is more, a headman usually had good hunting land and food-gathering sites which he shared with his group.

Atsugewi people were friendly to tribes around them, sharing hunting places. They did not have horses, so they were at the mercy of horse-riding tribes from the north, who often raided the Atsugewi tribe, taking them as slaves. Stone forts were built by the Atsugewi to protect themselves from raiders.

Tribal councils decided if a war was worth fighting, and a war was never waged very far away from home. When a battle was fought, both warring tribes faced each other in two long lines. A peacemaker tried to solve the problem at this time. If the matter could not be settled, the peacemaker would then step aside, and both sides shot arrows at each other until one side won.

A chief might or might not fight in a battle. If he did fight, neither side could touch him. If the chief wanted, he could stop the fight and arrange a settlement. A battle was directed by the best warrior. Unlike the protected chief, the enemy was allowed to kill the best warrior.

While a battle was being fought, the women at home did a war dance every morning and night. Women shouted for their men to do well in their battle, and baskets of water were thrown into the air for good luck.

When the warriors came home from fighting, village women drenched them with shredded epos roots to celebrate their return. Then a feast was held that evening with a war dance being performed.

During food-gathering time in the summer, large dinners, or feasts, could be given by the Atsugewi people. Other tribes were invited. The best kind of get-together was a "big time" party, which the chief called when he felt enough food for winter had been gathered.

Knotted strings, one knot for each day until the party, were sent to other villages and tribes by runners, inviting them to the celebration. The chief stood on his roof to welcome visitors on the day of the party.

Large baskets of food were given to a visiting chief for his people. For the next three or four days games of chance, wrestling, foot races, weight-lifting, bow-and-arrow contests, and stick games were played. Extra food was divided among the guests as they left the party.

Trading often took place during a "big-time" party. Trading was important to the tribe. It was one way of keeping close ties with nearby tribes. If money was needed to get something, Atsugewi people used clamshell money.

To make the money, tribal members filed clamshell pieces into small beads, all the same size, and strung them on vegetable-fiber strings. Although other tribes around them thought tiny dentalia shells were far more valuable, the Atsugewis considered the clamshell-bead money strings to be worth more than dentalia.

When a man chose a wife, he looked for a woman who worked hard. A young man might watch the young girls come in from gathering food, to see which of them carried the largest baskets of food. Then he could be sure of her ability to work well, if he should decide to marry her.

Women did all the food gathering and preparation. How much food was stored for the long, hard winters in Atsugewi territory depended upon the woman's ability to gather and prepare it. Life and death of a family depended on how able the woman was. That is why Atsugewi women were considered more valuable than men.

After a young couple decided to marry, gifts were exchanged between both sets of parents. This gift giving continued throughout the marriage. It was felt that gifts would always keep good feelings between both families.

A woman went to her own parents' home to give birth to her babies. Children were very much wanted and loved. A new mother's own mother made the baby's first cradle. When the baby was a bit older, a larger cradle was made. This cradle was pointed at the bottom so it could be stuck into the ground while the new mother gathered and prepared food.

A child's early training was very important to Atsugewi people. Lying and fighting were frowned upon. Disobedient

Twined basket with geometric design.

young children were spanked with a coyote tail. If a child really misbehaved, parents might pierce the unruly child's ears or duck the child in cold water. Stories were told to children about ghosts or spirits who did not like naughty children. Parents hoped this would scare their children into being good.

The tribe had a ceremony for girls when they became teenagers. The ceremony could last as long as six days. There were dances performed, and the girls had to work hard most of those days. In a summer ceremony, girls had to dig roots all day. In a winter ritual, a girl worked in the cookhouse for several days, never leaving except to carry in wood. At the end of the ceremony, a girl's ears were pierced to show she was now an adult woman.

Boys had a ceremony when their voices changed. They were given skunk-brush belts to wear. A boy's father, or a hard-working village man, spoke sternly to the young man about being a good adult. His ears were pierced, and he was whipped with either a bow string or a coyote tail; then he was sent away from the village on a three day search for power.

If the boy heard a fawn call to its mother during this search period, he believed he would have great hunting power as he grew older. Also while he was gone, a boy took it as a sign that he should be a doctor if he heard an old man groan.

31

CUSTOMS AND BELIEFS

There was one solid belief in an Atsugewi's life: The only way to success and wealth was by hard work. For this reason, ordinary tools and cooking utensils became the sign of a person's wealth within the tribe. The more objects a person owned that were useful, the richer that person was considered to be. Beads were the only useless form of "riches" an Atsugewi ever owned.

So serious were they about owning only useful things, they did not even prize fancy woodpecker feathers or pretty decorations like other tribes did.

Big objects, such as canoes, fishing nets, or pestles, could be borrowed from a village rich man; the loan was then repaid with small gifts of food to the owner when the object was returned.

Hard-working rich people were always looked up to by other villagers. Some rich men would work all night at a project, like making string, so villagers could show their children how hard they worked for their wealth. Children were taught not to be lazy, to be eager for work, and to get up early each day.

Women were never to gossip or eat while they gathered food and dug roots. They had to work far apart from each other so they would not take time away from work by talking. Men also were expected to work at all times. They even hunted in midwinter, when snow was deep.

Although the Atsugewi people visited Maidu tribal dances and parties, they did not give many themselves. They did have teenage ceremonies but even that ceremony was mainly about always being hard-working as adults. It was felt more time could be spent on food-gathering if the tribe did not have to prepare for ceremonies or feasts. That is why the few parties given were planned only when more than enough food had been gathered for the winter months.

Atsugewi people believed that if a man was accidentally killed by another person, that person had to make a payment of money to the dead man's family. The village chief made sure all payments were made. If a person was accidentally hurt, no money needed to be paid. But if someone was deliberately killed, then the murderer would have to take care of the dead man's family.

When a villager died, the body was dressed in its best buckskin clothes. It was placed with knees drawn up to its chin, tied into that position with leather thongs and wrapped in a skin blanket. If the dead person was not a chief or a rich man, the body was buried among lava rocks located far from the village.

A chief or rich man, however, was usually buried in the floor of his earth lodge home, and the lodge was then burned. Belongings sometimes were put in the grave with the body. Close relatives of the dead person went into a long period of mourning. During this time, they would cut off their hair and cover their heads with soot, chalk, and tree pitch. The widow made a belt from her cut hair and wore it while she was in mourning.

RELIGION

The Atsugewis felt god-spirits of nature had great power over them. They believed these spirits might take the form of a human, as well as an animal. If someone had bad luck, the luck was blamed on that villager's unhappy guardian spirit. It was felt tribal members should always have a spirit or two to keep them lucky and in good health.

Atsugewi people believed that if a spirit liked a human, it sang to that person. If the human sang the same one back to the spirit, then that particular song could always be used to call to the spirit for help. Other songs were practiced, either alone in the hills or with other tribe members in the winter lodge. Singing was a major part of Atsugewi life.

Pain was considered the main reason for illness. Therefore, it was pain that had to be removed from the bodies of sick people before they could begin to heal.

Atsugewis believed that angry spirit-gods caused pain to enter the body of a human who had not been good. It was felt that if the kind of pain causing a sickness was discovered, it should then be taken from the sick person and sent back to the guardian spirit to be killed.

A shaman, or spirit-doctor, was thought by villagers to be more powerful, and to have many more personal spirits, than regular tribal members. Villagers depended upon the shamans' strong spirit powers to draw the pain from a sick person into their own bodies. From there, it was felt, the pain could more easily be sent back to a person's guardian spirit to be killed.

Shamans, who were like magicians today, used many objects to symbolize pain. Their pain objects could be anything from the whisker of a guardian-spirit animal (a small hair) to the whole spirit-animal itself (a snake or dead animal). Splinters of wood, a piece of stone, flies, or bear claws were made to magically appear to from the sick human's body by shamans.

Pain was divided into 15 or 20 kinds, and a shaman had songs for each pain. It often took five years of training to perfectly learn the songs of the tribe's kinds of pain. These songs would be sung during healing rituals.

Sometimes a shaman's pain ritual could go on for two or three nights. When a villager was very ill, the shaman would wear a special feather headdress during the ritual. Each feather in the headdress symbolized one of the pains. If, after many days of singing and dancing, the pain could still not be found, and removed from the sick person, a shaman from another village or tribe was often brought in to help with the curing.

All of the shaman ceremonies were more of a "magic" show than anything else. People usually knew this, but wanted to believe in guardian spirits, anyway.

HUNTING AND FISHING

In the summer months, Atsugewi land had a great deal of water. Much water meant all kinds of food to eat. Not only fish, but animals and plants could be gathered during the warm weather. In spite of the tribe's worry about not having enough food, there were things they did not eat. Some foods

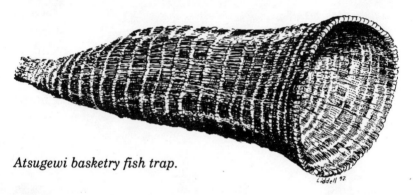

Atsugewi basketry fish trap.

could not be eaten for religious reasons, and some just did not taste good to tribal members. They did not eat mink, gray fox, coyote, frog, eagle, buzzard, magpie, or crow.

Fish was a mainstay of Atsugewi meals. All kinds of fish, except salmon were found in the streams near villages. Salmon could be caught on the Pit River, but only by invitation of the Achumewi tribe. Men were in charge of most of the fishing; what little fishing women did was only with a hook and line.

Some fish were caught in loosely woven basket traps. An especially good one Atsugewi fishermen used was an open-twined basket trap that looked like a giant five-foot-long ice cream cone.

Village men spent many hours making and mending nets of a heavy vegetable-fiber string. Gill nets were hung vertically in the water, catching fish by their gills as they tried to swim through the nets. A dip net was made of netting attached to a small tree branch, which was bent into a circle. Handles were attached to the net so the fishermen could stay on the bank and scoop fish out of a stream from shore.

Fish could be speared from a canoe at night, using torches as light to attract the fish. Atsugewi canoes were made from pine, cedar, or fir logs. The inside of a log was burned or chopped out to make it into a boat. This kind of boat did not have much shape but floated well. Fishing at night, by torchlight, is still done by fishermen today.

All kinds of methods and equipment were used to catch fish. Sometimes baskets were simply hung from tree branches over a waterfall to catch fish. Other times fish in quiet pools were hit with bundles of wild parsley to stun them, so they could be lifted right out of the water.

Women prepared the fish for eating. Usually it was cooked over an open fire. Those fish not eaten right away were split in two, dried, then stored in small baskets for winter meals.

Deer meat, or venison, was not as important a tribal food as fish. It was considered to be food only for the rich villagers. Although men usually hunted alone for deer or antelope, once in a while several men, led by a chief, would hunt together. The night before would then be spent singing power songs and planning the hunt.

One method of hunting in a group was to set fires, causing the deer or antelope to rush past other hunters waiting with bows and arrows ready. As many as fifteen animals could be killed this way during a big hunt.

Another way of group hunting was to sing songs to charm the animals so they could be surrounded and killed more easily. A long rope made of tule was used to circle the group of deer or antelope that had been charmed by the singing. Bows and arrows were then used to kill the animals.

Meat from one of the big hunts was always shared with the chief and his relatives. Even when men hunted alone, meat was given to the chief to divide among the people of the tribe. Extra meat was smoked or dried on long poles strung between trees. It was then stored in pits, or in baskets hung in trees, to keep animals from reaching it.

Lone hunters sometimes chased a deer until it was tired enough to be trapped. Single hunters also could shoot a passing deer from a hidden place near a deer trail. Another way for one man to hunt alone was to follow deer while wearing a deer head on his own head. This way the hunter could get closer to deer without being noticed by them.

Often men would use a grass stem to imitate the sound of a fawn calling to its mother. This might bring the mother deer closer to the hunter. Single hunters could use rope, snares, or pits to catch unaware deer. The Pit River got its name from these pits Native Americans dug to catch deer.

When a hunter was after a grizzly bear, he used poisonous arrow tips. Any hunter who killed a bear was felt to be the best hunter of all.

A group of hunters might drive many rabbits into a snare net. Sometimes hunters spread out in one line and moved into a large area. As they moved they would kill every animal that started running ahead of them. Special arrows and nets were used to catch birds. Ducks and mud hens were eaten, or dried for winter storage.

It is important to know that all animal hunting was for food or clothing. Native Americans did not hunt for fun, as many people do today. Nothing of an animal was wasted. The skin was used for clothing; bones were used for tools and whistles; meat was eaten; tendons became strong, stretchy string for the making of tools and bows.

Tribespeople ate more than 100 kinds of plants. Acorns were the most important plant food to the Atsugewi people, even though few oak trees grew in their territory. Some tribelets traveled long distances to oak tree groves to gather the acorn nuts. Men of the tribelets would climb trees and knock acorns to the ground. The acorns were then loaded into baskets and taken home, basket by basket. They were stored in special bark bins, or in pits, until needed the following winter.

Besides acorns, other important plant foods were epos and camass roots, and five kinds of sunflower seeds. Most of these were dried for storage. After roots and nuts were dried, they were ground up on mortars, with basket hoppers attached, to make flour. The flour then could be made into cakes in earth ovens. Mush was made by adding water to the flour, placing it in a basket with hot rocks, and tossing the rocks inside the basket until the mush was cooked.

HISTORY

The Atsugewi tribe lived so far away from the coast that they did not have to deal with white people until much later than most other California Native American tribes. It was not until about 1830 that a Hudson Bay trading company from Canada began trapping animals along lakes, creeks, and river banks in Atsugewi territory. These trappers were on their way to the Sacramento Valley. Gold miners came later, in 1851, followed by American settlers.

In 1856, tribal warriors attacked white people who had settled on Atsugewi land, killing some of them. The settlers fought back, and a fort was built by the United States government, in 1857, to prevent more land problems between Native Americans and the settlers.

Nevertheless, trouble continued between the settlers and tribal people. Finally, in 1859, a whole village of innocent Atsugewi were killed. White settlers thought the innocent tribe had killed some white people at Hat Creek.

After that sad mistake, all Native Americans were rounded up by the United States government and taken to Round Valley Reservation near the California coast. The Native Americans were so outnumbered by white people that they could no longer protect their land. Their attempts at trying to regain some of their sacred areas and food gathering sites were not understood by government. The Atsugewis were looked upon as troublemakers.

Through the following years, the Atsugewis began moving back, one by one, to their old territory. In time, the government gave small plots of land in Dixie Valley and along Hat Creek to those who returned.

Those Atsugewi continued to gather their native foods and to use shamans. Some worked for white farmers and ranchers. Some worked in saw mills in the area. One of their earth-covered dance houses was still partly standing in the 1940s.

In 1972 there were five or six families still living on the old Hat Creek land given to them by the government over 100 years ago. There is still a bit of Atsugewi land in Burney and in Susanville, CA. Not too long ago, Atsugewi women began, once again, to make baskets and cradles, but very little of the Atsugewi culture remains today.

ATSUGEWI TRIBE OUTLINE

I. Introduction
    A. Two groups of people
    B. Meaning of name
II. The land
    A. Description of land
    B. Boundary problems
III. The village
    A. Number of buildings in smaller villages
    B. 1880 sweathouse description
    C. Larger villages and clustering
    D. Best locations for villages
IV. Village life
    A. Chiefs
        1. Only village chiefs
        2. Usually rich
        3. Most were very powerful
        4. Duties
        5. Paid for village feasts
        6. New chief usually son of old one
        7. Day of rest called by chief
    B. Sweat dances before winter hunt
    C. Village wealthy men and friends
    D. Slave-raiding northern tribes
        1. Stone forts
    E. War
        1. Tribal council decision
        2. Safety of chief in battle
        3. Women's war dance

F. "Big-time" party and trading
    1. Invitations of knotted strings
    2. Games and contests
    3. String money
G. Marriage
    1. Man's responsibilities
    2. Women's duties
    3. Gift exchange of families
H. Childbirth customs
I. Child training
    1. Punishment given
J. Teenage boys' and girls' ceremonies

V. Customs and beliefs
A. Hard work
B. Wealth and useful tools
C. Loan of large objects from wealthy people
D. Little time allowed for parties or conversation
E. Penalties for crimes
F. Death and mourning customs

VI. Religion
A. God-spirits as guardians
B. Guardian-spirit song
C. Shamans
    1. Pain and its curing
    2. Rituals and costumes

VII. Hunting and fishing
A. Animals not eaten
B. Fishing
    1. Traps and nets
    2. Permission for salmon
    3. Canoes and spear fishing
    4. Cooking preparations and storing of fish

C. Hunting
   1. Unimportance of animal meat
   2. Food of the rich
   3. Group hunting
   4. Hunting alone
   5. Using sounds to hunt
   6. Using all of an animal for tribe's needs
D. Food gathering
   1. Acorns, roots, grasses

VIII. History
   A. First encounter with white people
   B. Troubles with white settlers
   C. United States government reservations
   D. Small bits of Atsugewi land returned to them, finally
   E. How many families still on living on land from government
   F. Little remaining of culture

GLOSSARY

AWL: a sharp, pointed tool used for making small holes in leather or wood

CEREMONY: a meeting of people to perform formal rituals for a special reason; like an awards ceremony to hand out trophies to those who earned honors

CHERT: rock which can be chipped off, or flaked, into pieces with sharp edges

COILED: a way of weaving baskets which looks like the basket is made of rope coils woven together

DIAMETER: the length of a straight line through the center of a circle

DOWN: soft, fluffy feathers

DROUGHT: a long period of time without water

DWELLING: a building where people live

FLETCHING: attaching feathers to the back end of an arrow to make the arrow travel in a straight line

GILL NET: a flat net hanging vertically in water to catch fish by their heads and gills

GRANARIES: basket-type storehouses for grains and nuts

HERITAGE: something passed down to people from their long-ago relatives

LEACHING: washing away a bitter taste by pouring water through foods like acorn meal

MORTAR: flat surface of wood or stone used for the grinding of grains or herbs with a pestle

PARCHING:	to toast or shrivel with dry heat
PESTLE:	a small stone club used to mash, pound, or grind in a mortar
PINOLE:	flour made from ground corn
INDIAN RESERVATION:	land set aside for Native Americans by the United States government
RITUAL:	a ceremony that is always performed the same way
SEINE NET:	a net which hangs vertically in the water, encircling and trapping fish when it is pulled together
SHAMAN:	tribal religious men or women who use magic to cure illness and speak to spirit-gods
SINEW:	stretchy animal tendons
STEATITE:	a soft stone (soapstone) mined on Catalina Island by the Gabrielino tribe; used for cooking pots and bowls
TABOO:	something a person is forbidden to do
TERRITORY:	land owned by someone or by a group of people
TRADITION:	the handing down of customs, rituals, and belief, by word of mouth or example, from generation to generation
TREE PITCH:	a sticky substance found on evergreen tree bark
TWINING:	a method of weaving baskets by twisting fibers, rather than coiling them around a support fiber

NATIVE AMERICAN WORDS
WE KNOW AND USE

PLANTS AND TREES
hickory
pecan
yucca
mesquite
saguaro

ANIMALS
caribou
chipmunk
cougar
jaguar
opossum
moose

STATES
Dakota – friend
Ohio – good river
Minnesota – waters that
  reflect the sky
Oregon – beautiful water
Nebraska – flat water
Arizona
Texas

FOODS
avocado
hominy
maize (corn)
persimmon
tapioca
succotash

GEOGRAPHY
bayou – marshy body of
  water
savannah – grassy plain
pasadena – valley

WEATHER
blizzard
Chinook (warm, dry wind)

FURNITURE
hammock

HOUSE
wigwam
wickiup
tepee
igloo

INVENTIONS
toboggan

BOATS
canoe
kayak

OTHER WORDS
caucus – group meeting
mugwump – loner politician
squaw – woman
papoose – baby

CLOTHING
moccasin
parka
mukluk – slipper
poncho

BIBLIOGRAPHY

Cressman, L. S. *Prehistory of the Far West.* Salt Lake City, Utah: University of Utah Press, 1977.

Heizer, Robert F., volume editor. *Handbook of North American Indians; California, volume 8.* Washington, D.C.: Smithsonian Institute, 1978.

Heizer, Robert F. and Elsasser, Albert B. *The Natural World of the California Indians.* Berkeley and Los Angeles, CA; London, England: University of California Press, 1980.

Heizer, Robert F. and Whipple, M.A.. *The California Indians.* Berkeley and Los Angeles, CA; London, England: University of California Press, 1971.

Heuser, Iva. *California Indians.* PO Box 352, Camino, CA 95709: Sierra Media Systems, 1977.

Macfarlen, Allen and Paulette. *Handbook of American Indian Games.* 31 E. 2nd Street, Mineola, N.Y. 11501: Dover Publications, 1985.

Murphey, Edith Van Allen. *Indian Uses of Native Plants.* 603 W. Perkins Street, Ukiah, CA 95482: Mendocino County Historical Society, © renewal, 1987.

National Geographic Society. *The World of American Indians.* Washington, DC: National Geographic Society reprint, 1989.

Tunis, Edwin. *Indians.* 2231 West 110th Street, Cleveland, OH: The World Publishing Company, 1959.

Weatherford, Jack. *Native Roots.* 201 E. 50th., New York, N.Y.: Crown Publishers, Inc. 1991.

Credits:
Island Industries, Vashon Island, Washington 98070
Dona McAdam, Mac on the Hill, Seattle, Washington 98109

Acknowledgements:
Richard Buchen, Research Librarian, Braun Library,
Southwest Museum
Special thanks

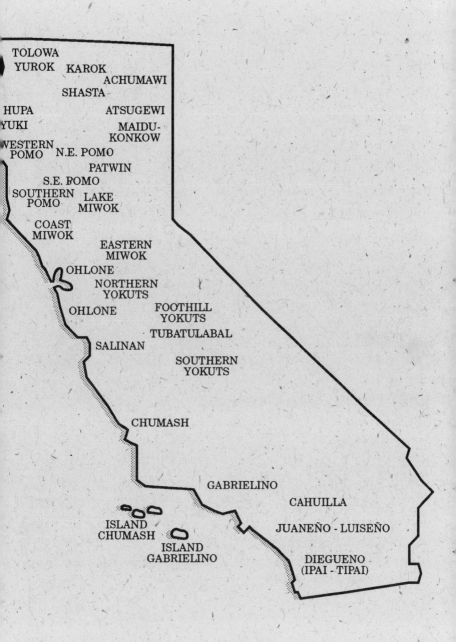

TOLOWA
YUROK   KAROK
            ACHUMAWI
         SHASTA
HUPA   ATSUGEWI
YUKI   MAIDU-
            KONKOW
WESTERN
POMO   N.E. POMO
         PATWIN
    S.E. POMO
SOUTHERN   LAKE
    POMO   MIWOK
    COAST
    MIWOK
         EASTERN
          MIWOK
    OHLONE
         NORTHERN
          YOKUTS
    OHLONE
         FOOTHILL
          YOKUTS
         TUBATULABAL
    SALINAN
         SOUTHERN
          YOKUTS

         CHUMASH

              GABRIELINO
                   CAHUILLA
    ISLAND   JUANEÑO - LUISEÑO
    CHUMASH
       ISLAND
       GABRIELINO   DIEGUENO
                    (IPAI - TIPAI)

Map Art: Dona McAdam

At last, a detailed book on the Atsugewi Tribe written just for students

Mary Null Boulé taught in the California public school system for twenty-five years. Her teaching years made her aware of the acute need for well-researched regional social studies books for elementary school students. This series on the California Native American tribes fills a long-standing need in California education. Ms. Boulé is also author and publisher of *The Missions: California's Heritage*. She is married and the mother of five grown children.

Illustrator Daniel Liddell has been creating artistic replicas of Native American artifacts for several years, and his paintings reflect his own Native American heritage. His paternal grandmother was full-blood Chickasaw.

ISBN: 1-877599-26-3